Java Quick Syntax Reference

Mikael Olsson

Apress*

Java Quick Syntax Reference

ISBN-13 (pbk): 978-1-4302-6286-2

ISBN-13 (electronic): 978-1-4302-6287-9

Distributed to the book trade worldwide by Springer Science+Business Media New York, 233 Spring Street, 6th Floor, New York, NY 10013. Phone 1-800-SPRINGER, fax (201) 348-4505, e-mail orders-ny@springer-sbm.com, or visit www.springeronline.com. Apress Media, LLC is a California LLC and the sole member (owner) is Springer Science + Business Media Finance Inc (SSBM Finance Inc). SSBM Finance Inc is a **Delaware** corporation.

For information on translations, please e-mail rights@apress.com, or visit www.apress.com.

Apress and friends of ED books may be purchased in bulk for academic, corporate, or promotional use. eBook versions and licenses are also available for most titles. For more information, reference our Special Bulk Sales–eBook Licensing web page at www.apress.com/bulk-sales.

Any source code or other supplementary material referenced by the author in this text is available to readers at www.apress.com. For detailed information about how to locate your book's source code, go to www.apress.com/source-code/.

Contents at a Glance

About the Author xi

Introduction xiii

Chapter 1: Hello World 1

Chapter 2: Compile and Run 3

Chapter 3: Variables 5

Chapter 4: Operators 9

Chapter 5: String 13

Chapter 6: Arrays 15

Chapter 7: Conditionals 19

Chapter 8: Loops... 21

Chapter 9: Methods 25

Chapter 10: Class 29

Chapter 11: Static.. 35

Chapter 12: Inheritance.. 39

Chapter 13: Overriding 41

Chapter 14: Packages and Import 45

Chapter 15: Access Levels.. 47

Chapter 16: Constants 51

Chapter 17: Interface.. 53

▓Chapter 18: Abstract **57**

▓Chapter 19: Enum **59**

▓Chapter 20: Exception Handling **61**

▓Chapter 21: Boxing and Unboxing **65**

▓Chapter 22: Generics **67**

Index **73**

Contents

About the Author xi

Introduction xiii

Chapter 1: Hello World 1

Installing 1

Creating a project 1

Hello world 1

Code hints 2

Chapter 2: Compile and Run 3

Running from the IDE 3

Running from a console window 3

Comments 4

Chapter 3: Variables 5

Data types 5

Declaring variables 5

Assigning variables 6

Using variables 6

Integer types 6

Floating-point types 7

Char type 7

Boolean type 7

Variable scope 8

Anonymous block 8

▨Chapter 4: Operators 9

Arithmetic operators 9

Assignment operators 9

Combined assignment operators 9

Increment and decrement operators................................ 10

Comparison operators 10

Logical operators.. 11

Bitwise operators 11

Operator precedence... 11

▨Chapter 5: String 13

Combining strings 13

Escape characters 13

String compare.. 14

StringBuffer class... 14

▨Chapter 6: Arrays 15

Array declaration... 15

Array allocation 15

Array assignment 15

Multi-dimensional arrays 16

ArrayList class.. 16

▓**Chapter 7: Conditionals** **19**

If statement 19

Switch statement 20

Ternary operator 20

▓**Chapter 8: Loops** **21**

While loop 21

Do-while loop 21

For loop 21

Foreach loop 22

Break and continue 22

Labeled block 23

▓**Chapter 9: Methods** **25**

Defining methods 25

Calling methods 25

Method parameters 25

Return statement 26

Method overloading 27

Passing arguments 27

▓**Chapter 10: Class** **29**

Object creation 29

Accessing object members 29

Constructor 30

This keyword 31

Constructor overloading 31

Constructor chaining 32

Initial field values 32

Default constructor 32

Null 32

Default values 33

Garbage collector 33

Chapter 11: Static **35**

Accessing static members 35

Static methods 36

Static fields 36

Static initialization blocks 36

Initialization blocks 37

Chapter 12: Inheritance **39**

Object 39

Upcasting 39

Downcasting 40

Instanceof operator 40

Chapter 13: Overriding **41**

Overriding members 41

Override annotation 41

Hiding members 42

Preventing method inheritance 43

Accessing overridden methods 43

Calling parent constructor 43

Chapter 14: Packages and Import **45**

Import specific class 45

Import package 46

Import static 46

Chapter 15: Access Levels...**47**

Private access 47

Package-private access 48

Protected access... 48

Public access 48

Top-level access.. 49

Nested class access... 49

Access level guideline.. 49

Chapter 16: Constants **51**

Local constants 51

Constant fields 51

Constant method parameters... 52

Compile-time and run-time constants 52

Constant guideline 52

Chapter 17: Interface...**53**

Interface members... 53

Interface example 54

Functionality interface.. 55

Class interface 55

Interface classes 56

Chapter 18: Abstract **57**

Abstract class example 57

Abstract classes and interfaces 58

Abstract class and interface guideline.................................... 58

▓Chapter 19: Enum **59**

Enum example 59

Enum class 60

▓Chapter 20: Exception Handling **61**

Try-catch 61

Catch block 61

Finally block 62

Throwing exceptions 62

Checked and unchecked exceptions 63

Exception hierarchy 63

▓Chapter 21: Boxing and Unboxing **65**

Autoboxing and autounboxing 65

Primitive and wrapper guideline 66

▓Chapter 22: Generics **67**

Generic classes 67

Generic methods 68

Calling generic methods 68

Generic interfaces 69

Generic type parameters 69

Generic variable usages 70

Bounded type parameters 70

Generics and Object 71

Index **73**

About the Author

Mikael Olsson is a professional web entrepreneur, programmer, and author. He works for an R&D company in Finland where he specializes in software development. In his spare time he writes books and creates websites that summarize various fields of interest. The books he writes are focused on teaching their subject in the most efficient way possible, by explaining only what is relevant and practical without any unnecessary repetition or theory.

Introduction

Java is a high-level object-oriented programming language developed by Sun Microsystems, which became part of Oracle Corporation in 2010. The language is very similar to C++, but has been simplified to make it easier to write bug free code. Most notably, there are no pointers in Java, instead all memory allocation and deallocation is handled automatically.

Despite simplifications like this Java has considerably more functionality than both C and C++, due to its large class library. Java programs also have high performance and can be made very secure, which has contributed to making Java the most popular general purpose programming language in use today.

Another key feature of Java is that it is platform independent. This is achieved by only compiling programs half-way, into platform independent instructions called bytecode. The bytecode is then interpreted, or run, by the Java Virtual Machine (JVM). This means that any system that has this program and its accompanying libraries installed can run Java applications.

There are three class libraries available for the Java programming language: Java ME, Java SE and Java EE. Java ME (Mobile Edition) is a stripped down version of Java SE (Standard Edition), while Java EE (Enterprise Edition) is an extended version of Java SE that includes libraries for building web applications.

The Java language and class libraries have undergone major changes since their initial release in 1996. The naming conventions for the versions have gone through a few revisions as well. The major releases include: JDK 1.0, JDK 1.1, J2SE 1.2, J2SE 1.3, J2SE 1.4, J2SE 5.0, Java SE 6 and Java SE 7, which is the current version as of writing.

After J2SE 1.4 the version number was changed from 1.5 to 5.0 for marketing reasons. As of J2SE 5.0, there is one version number for the product and another one used internally by the developers. J2SE 5.0 is the product name, while Java 1.5 is the developer version. Similarly, Java SE 7 is the product and Java 1.7 the internal version number. For simplicity's sake, the Java versions will be referred to as Java 1-7 in this book. Note that Java is designed to be backwards compatible. Thus the Virtual Machine for Java 7 can still run Java 1 class files.

CHAPTER 1

Hello World

Installing

Before you can program in Java you need to download and install the Java Development Kit (JDK) Standard Edition (SE) from Oracle's website.[1] Among other things, the JDK includes the Java compiler, the class libraries and the virtual machine needed to run Java applications. Oracle's download page also has a link to obtain Netbeans[2] bundled with the JDK. Netbeans is an Integrated Development Environment (IDE) that will make development in Java much easier. Alternatively, another free IDE you can use is Eclipse,[3] or if you do not want to use any IDE at all a regular text editor will work just fine.

Creating a project

If you decide to use an IDE (recommended) you need to create a project, which will manage the Java source files and other resources. Alternatively, if you prefer not to use an IDE you can create an empty file with the .java extension, for example MyApp.java, and open it in your text editor of choice.

    To create a project in Netbeans, go to the File menu and select New Project. From the dialog box select the Java Application project type under the Java category and click next. On this dialog box set the project name to "MyProject" and the name of the main class to "myproject.MyApp". Change the project's location if you want to, and then hit the Finish button to generate the project. The project's only file, MyApp.java, will then open up, containing some default code. You can go ahead and remove all of that code so that you start with an empty source file.

Hello world

When you have your project and programming environment set up the first application you will create is the Hello World program. This program will teach you how to compile and run Java applications, as well as how to output a string to a command window.

---

[1] http://www.oracle.com/technetwork/java/javase/downloads/index.html
[2] http://www.netbeans.org
[3] http://www.eclipse.org

The first step in creating this program is to add a public class to your MyApp.java source file. The class must have the same name as the physical source file without the file extension, in this case "MyApp". It is legal to have more than one class per file in Java, but only one public class is allowed, and that name must match the filename. Keep in mind that Java is case sensitive. The curly brackets following the class name delimits what belongs to the class and must be included. The brackets, along with their content, is referred to as a code block, or just a block.

```
public class MyApp {}
```

Next, add the main method inside the class. This is the starting point of the application and must always be included in the same form as is shown below. The keywords themselves will be looked at in later chapters.

```
public class MyApp {
  public static void main(String[] args) {}
}
```

The last step in completing the Hello World program is to output the text by calling the print method. This method is located inside the built-in System class, and then another level down inside the out class. The method takes a single argument – the string to be printed – and it ends with a semicolon, as do all statements in Java.

```
public class MyApp {
  public static void main(String[] args) {
    System.out.print("Hello World");
  }
}
```

Note that the dot operator (.) is used to access members of a class.

Code hints

If you are unsure of what a specific class contains, or what arguments a method takes, you can take advantage of code hints in some IDEs, such as Netbeans. The code hint window appears anytime you are typing code and there are multiple predetermined alternatives. It can also be brought up manually by pressing Ctrl + Space. This is a very powerful feature that gives you quick access to the whole class library and their members, along with descriptions.

CHAPTER 2

■ ■ ■

Compile and Run

Running from the IDE

With your Hello World program complete you can compile and run it in one of two ways. The first method is by selecting run from the menu bar of the IDE that you are using. In Netbeans the menu command is: Run ➤ Run Main Project. The IDE will then compile and run the application, which displays the text "Hello World".

Running from a console window

The other way is to manually compile the program by using a console window (C:\Windows\System32\cmd.exe). The most convenient way to do this is to first add the JDK bin directory to the PATH environment variable. In Windows, this can be done by using the SET PATH command, and then by appending the path to your JDK installation's bin folder separated by a semicolon.

```
SET PATH=%PATH%;"C:\Program Files\JDK\bin"
```

By doing this the console will be able to find the Java compiler from any folder for the duration of this console session. The PATH variable can also be permanently changed.[1] Next, navigate to the folder where the source file is located and run the compiler by typing "javac" followed by the complete filename.

```
javac MyApp.java
```

The program will be compiled into a class file called MyApp.class. This class file contains bytecode instead of machine code, so to execute it you need to call the Java Virtual Machine by typing "java" followed by the filename.

```
java MyApp
```

Notice that the .java extension is used when compiling a file, but the .class extension is not used when running it.

---

[1] http://www.java.com/en/download/help/path.xml

Comments

Comments are used to insert notes into the source code and will have no effect on the end program. Java has the standard C++ comment notation, with both single-line and multi-line comments.

```
// single-line comment

/* multi-line
   comment */
```

In addition to these, there is the Javadoc comment. This comment is used to generate documentation by using a utility included in the JDK bin folder which is also called Javadoc.

```
/** javadoc
   comment */
```

CHAPTER 3

Variables

Variables are used for storing data during program execution.

Data types

Depending on what data you need to store there are several kinds of data types. Java has eight types that are built into the language. These are called *primitives*. The integer (whole number) types are byte, short, int and long. The float and double types represent floating-point numbers (real numbers). The char type holds a Unicode character and the boolean type contains either a true or false value. Except for these primitive types, every other type in Java is represented by either a class, an interface or an array.

Data Type	Size (bits)	Description
byte	8	Signed integer
short	16	
int	32	
long	64	
float	32	Floating-point number
double	64	
char	16	Unicode character
boolean	1	Boolean value

Declaring variables

To declare (create) a variable you start with the data type you want it to hold followed by a variable name. The name can be anything you want, but it is a good idea to give your variables names that are closely related to the values they will hold. The standard naming convention for variables is that the first word should be lowercase and any subsequent words initially capitalized.

```
int myInt;
```

Assigning variables

To give the variable a value you use the assignment operator (=) followed by the value. When a variable is initialized (assigned a value) it then becomes defined (declared and assigned).

```
myInt = 10;
```

The declaration and assignment can be combined into a single statement.

```
int myInt = 10;
```

If you need multiple variables of the same type, there is a shorthand way of declaring or defining them by using the comma operator (,).

```
int myInt = 10, myInt2 = 20, myInt3;
```

Using variables

Once a variable has been defined it can be used by simply referencing the variable's name, for example to print it.

```
System.out.print(myInt);
```

Integer types

As shown earlier, there are four signed integer types that can be used depending on how large a number you need the variable to hold.

```
byte  myInt8  = 2;  // -128    to +127
short myInt16 = 1;  // -32768 to +32767
int   myInt32 = 0;  // -2^31   to +2^31-1
long  myInt64 = -1; // -2^63   to +2^63-1
```

In addition to standard decimal notation, integers can also be assigned by using octal or hexadecimal notation.

```
int myHex = 0xF; // hexadecimal (base 16)
int myOct = 07;  // octal (base 8)
```

Floating-point types

The floating-point types can store integers as well as floats. They can be assigned with either decimal or exponential notation.

```
double myDouble = 3.14;
double myDouble2 = 3e2; // 3*10^2 = 300
```

Note that constant floating-point numbers in Java are always kept internally as doubles. Therefore, if you try to assign a double to a float you will get an error, because a double has a higher precision than a float. To assign it correctly you can append an "F" character to the constant, which says that the number is in fact a float.

```
float myFloat = 3.14;  // error: possible loss
                       // of precision
float myFloat = 3.14F; // ok
```

A more common and useful way to do this is by using an explicit cast. An explicit cast is performed by placing the desired data type in parentheses before the variable or constant that is to be converted. This will convert the value to the specified type, in this case float, before the assignment occurs.

```
float myFloat = (float)3.14;
```

Char type

The char data type can contain a single Unicode character, delimited by single quotes.

```
char myChar = 'A';
```

Chars can also be assigned by using a special hexadecimal notation that gives access to all Unicode characters.

```
char myChar = '\u0000'; // \u0000 to \uFFFF
```

Boolean type

The boolean type can store a Boolean value, which is a value that can only be either true or false. These values are specified with the true and false keywords.

```
boolean myBool = false;
```

Variable scope

The scope of a variable refers to the code block within which it is possible to use that variable without qualification. For example, a local variable is a variable declared within a method. Such a variable will only be available within the method's code block, after it has been declared. Once the scope (code block) of the method ends, the local variable will be destroyed.

```
public static void main(String[] args)
{
  int localVar; // local variable
}
```

In addition to local variables, Java has field and parameter type variables, which will be looked at in later chapters. Java does not, however, have global variables, as for example does C++.

Anonymous block

The scope of local variables can be restricted by using an anonymous (unnamed) code block. This construct is seldom used, because if a method is large enough to warrant the use of an anonymous block, a better choice is often to break up the code into separate methods.

```
public static void main(String[] args)
{
  // Anonymous code block
  {
    int localVar = 10;
  }
  // localVar is unavailable from here
}
```

CHAPTER 4

Operators

Operators are used to operate on values. They can be grouped into five types: arithmetic, assignment, comparison, logical and bitwise operators.

Arithmetic operators

There are the four basic arithmetic operators, as well as the modulus operator (%) which is used to obtain the division remainder.

```
float x = 3+2; // 5 // addition
      x = 3-2; // 1 // subtraction
      x = 3*2; // 6 // multiplication
      x = 3/2; // 1 // division
      x = 3%2; // 1 // modulus (division remainder)
```

Notice that the division sign gives an incorrect result. This is because it operates on two integer values and will therefore round the result and return an integer. To get the correct value, one of the numbers must be explicitly converted to a floating-point type.

```
float x = (float)3/2; // 1.5
```

Assignment operators

The second group is the assignment operators. Most importantly, the assignment operator (=) itself, which assigns a value to a variable.

Combined assignment operators

A common use of the assignment and arithmetic operators is to operate on a variable and then to save the result back into that same variable. These operations can be shortened with the combined assignment operators.

```
int x = 0;
    x += 5; // x = x+5;
    x -= 5; // x = x-5;
    x *= 5; // x = x*5;
    x /= 5; // x = x/5;
    x %= 5; // x = x%5;
```

Increment and decrement operators

Another common operation is to increment or decrement a variable by one. This can be simplified with the increment (++) and decrement (--) operators.

```
++x; // x += 1
--x; // x -= 1
```

Both of these can be used either before or after a variable.

```
++x; // pre-increment
--x; // pre-decrement
x++; // post-increment
x--; // post-decrement
```

The result on the variable is the same whichever is used. The difference is that the post-operator returns the original value before it changes the variable, while the pre-operator changes the variable first and then returns the value.

```
x = 5; y = x++; // y=5, x=6
x = 5; y = ++x; // y=6, x=6
```

Comparison operators

The comparison operators compare two values and return either true or false. They are mainly used to specify conditions, which are expressions that evaluate to either true or false.

```
boolean x = (2==3); // false // equal to
        x = (2!=3); // true  // not equal to
        x = (2>3);  // false // greater than
        x = (2<3);  // true  // less than
        x = (2>=3); // false // greater than or equal to
        x = (2<=3); // true  // less than or equal to
```

Logical operators

The logical operators are often used together with the comparison operators. Logical and (&&) evaluates to true if both the left and right side are true, and logical or (||) is true if either the left or right side is true. For inverting a Boolean result there is the logical not (!) operator. Note that for both "logical and" and "logical or" the right-hand side will not be evaluated if the result is already determined by the left-hand side.

```
boolean x = (true && false); // false // logical and
        x = (true || false); // true  // logical or
        x = !(true);         // false // logical not
```

Bitwise operators

The bitwise operators can manipulate individual bits inside an integer. For example, the right shift operator (>>) moves all bits except the sign bit to the right, whereas zero-fill right shift (>>>) moves all bits right including the sign bit.

```
int x = 5 & 4; // 101 & 100 = 100 (4) // and
    x = 5 | 4; // 101 | 100 = 101 (5) // or
    x = 5 ^ 4; // 101 ^ 100 = 001 (1) // xor
    x = 4 << 1;// 100 << 1  =1000 (8) // left shift
    x = 4 >> 1;// 100 >> 1  =  10 (2) // right shift
    x = 4 >>>1;// 100 >>>1  =  10 (2) // zero-fill
                                      // right shift
    x = ~4;    // ~00000100 = 11111011 (-5) // invert
```

These bitwise operators have shorthand assignment operators, just like the arithmetic operators.

```
int x = 5;
    x  &= 5; // "and" and assign
    x  |= 5; // or and assign
    x  ^= 5; // xor and assign
    x <<= 5; // left shift and assign
    x >>= 5; // right shift and assign
    x>>>= 5; // right shift and assign (move sign bit)
```

Operator precedence

In Java, expressions are normally evaluated from left to right. However, when an expression contains multiple operators, the precedence of those operators decides the order that they are evaluated in. The order of precedence can be seen in the following table. This same order also applies to many other languages, such as C++ and C#.

Precedence	Operator	Precedence	Operator
1	++ --! ~	7	&
2	* / %	8	^
3	+ -	9	|
4	<< >> >>>	10	&&
5	< <= > >=	11	||
6	== !=	12	= op=

For example, logical and (&&) binds weaker than relational operators, which in turn binds weaker than arithmetic operators.

```
x = 2+3 > 1*4 && 5/5 == 1; // true
```

To avoid having to learn the precedents of all operators and to clarify the intent, parentheses can be used to specify which part of the expression will be evaluated first. Parentheses have the highest precedence of all operators.

```
x = ( (2+3) > (1*4) ) && ( (5/5) == 1 ); // true
```

CHAPTER 5

String

The String class in Java is a data type that can hold string literals. String is a reference data type, as are all non-primitive data types. This means that the variable contains an address to an object in the memory, and not the object itself. A String object is created in the memory, and the address to the object is returned to the variable.

As seen below, string literals are delimited by double quotes. This is actually a shorthand notation for the regular reference type initialization (creation) syntax, which uses the new keyword.

```
String a = "Hello";
String b = new String(" World");
```

Combining strings

The plus sign is used to combine two strings. It is known as the concatenation operator (+) in this context. The operator has an accompanying assignment operator (+=), which appends one string to another and creates a new string.

```
String c = a+b; // Hello World
        a += b;  // Hello World
```

Note that while a statement may be divided into multiple lines a string must be on a single row, unless it is split up by using the concatenation operator.

```
String x
        = "Hello " +
          "World";
```

Escape characters

For adding new lines to the string itself, there is the escape character "\n". This backslash notation is used to write special characters, such as backslash or double-quote. Among the special characters is also a Unicode character notation for writing any character. All of the escape characters can be seen in the following table.

Character	Meaning	Character	Meaning
\n	newline	\f	form feed
\t	horizontal tab	\'	single quote
\b	backspace	\"	double quote
\r	carriage return	\\	backslash
\uFFFF	Unicode character		
	(4-digit hex number)		

String compare

The way to compare two strings is by using the `equals` method of the `String` class. If the equality operator (`==`) is used, the memory addresses will be compared instead.

```
boolean x = a.equals(b); // compares string
boolean y = (a == b);    // compares address
```

Bear in mind that all strings in Java are `String` objects. Therefore, it is possible to call methods directly on constant strings, just as on variables.

```
boolean z = "Hello".equals(a);
```

StringBuffer class

The `String` class has a large number of methods available, but it does not contain any methods for manipulating strings. This is because strings in Java are immutable. Once a `String` object has been created the contents cannot be changed, unless the whole string is completely replaced. Since most strings are never modified this was done on purpose to make the `String` class more efficient. For cases when you need a modifiable string you can use the `StringBuffer` class, which is a mutable string object.

```
StringBuffer sb = new StringBuffer("Hello");
```

This class has several methods to manipulate strings, such as `append`, `delete` and `insert`.

```
sb.append(" World");   // add to end of string
sb.delete(0, 5);       // remove 5 first characters
sb.insert(0, "Hello"); // insert string at beginning
```

A `StringBuffer` object can be converted back into a regular string with the `toString` method.

```
String s = sb.toString();
```

CHAPTER 6

Arrays

An array is a data structure used for storing a collection of values.

Array declaration

To declare an array, a set of square brackets is appended to the data type the array will contain, followed by the array's name. Alternatively, the brackets may be placed after the array name. Arrays can be declared with any data type and all of its elements must then be of that type.

```
int[] x;
int y[];
```

Array allocation

The array is allocated with the new keyword, followed again by the data type and a set of square brackets containing the length of the array. This is the fixed number of elements that the array can contain. Once the array is created, the elements will automatically be assigned to the default values for that data type.

```
int y[] = new int[3];
```

Array assignment

To fill the array elements they can be referenced one at a time, by placing the element's index inside the square brackets, and then assigning them values. Notice that the index starts with zero.

```
y[0] = 1;
y[1] = 2;
y[2] = 3;
```

Alternatively, the values can be assigned all at once by using a curly bracket notation. The new keyword and data type may be optionally left out if the array is declared at the same time.

```
int[] x = new int[] {1,2,3};
int[] x = {1,2,3};
```

Once the array elements are initialized, they can be accessed by referencing the elements' indexes inside the square brackets.

```
System.out.print(x[0] + x[1] + x[2]); // 6
```

Multi-dimensional arrays

Multi-dimensional arrays are declared, created and initialized much like one-dimensional arrays, except that they have additional square brackets. They can have any number of dimensions, and for each dimension another set of square brackets is added.

```
String[][] x = {{"00","01"},{"10","11"}};
String[][] y = new String[2][2];

y[0][0] = "00";
y[0][1] = "01";
y[1][0] = "10";
y[1][1] = "11";

System.out.print(x[0][0] + x[1][1]); // "0011"
```

ArrayList class

An important thing to keep in mind about arrays is that their length is fixed and there are no methods available to change their size. In fact, the only array member that is regularly used is length, to obtain the size of the array.

```
int x[] = new int[3];
int size = x.length; // 3
```

For cases when a resizable array is needed the ArrayList class can be used, which is located in the java.util package. Items in the ArrayList are stored as the generic Object type. The ArrayList can therefore hold any data types, except for primitives.

```
// Create an Object ArrayList collection
java.util.ArrayList a = new java.util.ArrayList();
```

The ArrayList class has several useful methods to change the array, including: add, set and remove.

```
a.add("Hi");         // add an element
a.set(0, "Hello");   // change first element
a.remove(0);         // remove first element
```

To retrieve an element from the ArrayList the get method is used. The element then has to be explicitly cast back to its original type.

```
a.add("Hello World");
String s = (String)a.get(0); // Hello World
```

CHAPTER 7

Conditionals

Conditional statements are used to execute different code blocks based on different conditions.

If statement

The if statement will only execute if the condition inside the parentheses is evaluated to true. The condition can include any of the comparison and logical operators.

```
if (x < 1) {
   System.out.print(x + " < 1");
}
```

To test for other conditions, the if statement can be extended by any number of else if clauses. Each additional condition will only be tested if all previous conditions are false.

```
else if (x > 1) {
   System.out.print(x + " > 1");
}
```

The if statement can have one else clause at the end, which will execute if all previous conditions are false.

```
else {
   System.out.print(x + " == 1");
}
```

As for the curly brackets, they can be left out if only a single statement needs to be executed conditionally.

```
if (x < 1)
   System.out.print(x + " < 1");
else if (x > 1)
   System.out.print(x + " > 1");
else
   System.out.print(x + " == 1");
```

Switch statement

The switch statement checks for equality between an integer and a series of case labels. It then executes the matching case. The statement can contain any number of cases and may end with a default label for handling all other cases.

```
switch (y)
{
  case 0: System.out.print(y + " is 0"); break;
  case 1: System.out.print(y + " is 1"); break;
  default:System.out.print(y + " is something else");
}
```

Note that the statements after each case label are not surrounded by curly brackets. Instead, the statements end with the break keyword. Without the break the execution will fall through to the next case. This can be useful if several cases need to be evaluated in the same way.

The data types that can be used with a switch statement are: byte, short, int and char. As of Java 7, String types are also permitted.

Ternary operator

In addition to the if and switch statements there is the ternary operator (?:). This operator can replace a single if/else clause that assigns a value to a specific variable. The operator takes three expressions. If the first one is evaluated to true then the second expression is returned, and if it is false, the third one is evaluated and returned.

```
x = (x < 0.5) ? 0 : 1; // ternary operator (?:)
```

CHAPTER 8

Loops

There are four looping structures in Java. These are used to execute a specific code block multiple times. Just as with the conditional if statement, the curly brackets for the loops can be left out if there is only one statement in the code block.

While loop

The while loop runs through the code block only if the condition is true, and will continue looping for as long as the condition remains true. The loop below will print out the numbers 0 to 9.

```
int i = 0;
while (i < 10) { System.out.print(i++); }
```

Note that the condition for the loop is only checked at the start of each iteration (loop).

Do-while loop

The do-while loop works the same way as the while loop, except that it checks the condition after the code block. It will therefore always run through the code block at least once.

```
int i = 0;
do { System.out.print(i++); } while (i < 10);
```

For loop

The for loop is used to go through a code block a specific number of times. It uses three parameters. The first parameter initializes a counter and is always executed once, before the loop. The second parameter holds the condition for the loop and is checked before each iteration. The third parameter contains the increment of the counter and is executed at the end of each iteration.

```
for (int i = 0; i < 10; i++)
{ System.out.print(i); }
```

The for loop has several variations. For instance, the first and third parameters can be split into several statements by using the comma operator.

```
for (int k = 0, l = 10; k < 10; k++, l--)
{ System.out.print(k + l); }
```

There is also the option of leaving out one or more of the parameters. For example, the third parameter can be moved into the body of the loop.

```
for (int k = 0, l = 10; k < 10;)
{ System.out.print(k + l); k++, l--; }
```

Foreach loop

The foreach loop gives an easy way to iterate through arrays. On each iteration the next element in the array is assigned to the specified variable, and the loop continues to execute until it has gone through the entire array.

```
int[] array = { 1,2,3 };
for (int element : array) { System.out.print(element); }
```

Break and continue

There are two special keywords that can be used inside loops – break and continue. The break keyword ends the loop structure, and continue skips the rest of the current iteration and continues at the beginning of the next iteration.

```
break;    // end current loop
continue; // start next iteration
```

To break out of a loop above the current one, that loop must first be labeled by adding a name followed by a colon before it. With this label in place it can now be used as an argument to the break statement, telling it which loop to break out of. This also works with the continue keyword in order to skip to the next iteration of the named loop. Note that the continue statement in this example is unreachable because the previous break statement always prevents continue from executing.

```
myLoop: for (int i = 0, j = 0; i < 10; i++)
        {
          while (++j < 10)
          {
            break myLoop;    // end for
            continue myLoop; // start next for
          }
        }
```

Labeled block

A labeled block, also called a named block, is created by placing a label before an anonymous code block. The break keyword can be used to break out of such a block, just as in labeled loops. This could for example be useful when performing a validation, where if one validation step fails the whole process must be aborted.

```
validation:
{
  if(true)
    break validation;
}
```

Labeled blocks can be useful for organizing a large method into sections. In most cases though, splitting the method up is a better idea. However, if the new method would require a lot of parameters, or if the method would only be used from a single location, then one or more labeled blocks may be preferable.

CHAPTER 9

Methods

Methods are reusable code blocks that will only execute when called.

Defining methods

A method can be created by typing void followed by the method's name, a set of parentheses and a code block. The void keyword means that the method will not return a value. The naming convention for methods is the same as for variables – a descriptive name with the first word in lowercase and any other words initially capitalized.

```
class MyApp
{
  void myPrint()
  {
    System.out.print("Hello");
  }
}
```

Calling methods

The method above will simply print out a text message. To invoke (call) it from the main method an instance of the MyApp class must first be created. The dot operator is then used after the instance's name in order to access its members, which include the myPrint method.

```
public static void main(String[] args)
{
  MyApp m = new MyApp();
  m.myPrint(); // Hello
}
```

Method parameters

The parentheses that follow the method name are used to pass arguments to the method. To do this the corresponding parameters must first be added to the method declaration in the form of a comma separated list.

```
void myPrint(String s)
{
  System.out.print(s);
}
```

A method can be defined to take any number of arguments and they can have any data types, just ensure the method is called with the same types and number of arguments.

```
public static void main(String[] args)
{
  MyApp m = new MyApp();
  m.myPrint("Hello"); // Hello
}
```

To be precise, *parameters* appear in method definitions, while *arguments* appear in method calls. However, the two terms are sometimes used interchangeably.

Return statement

A method can return a value. The void keyword is then replaced with the data type the method will return, and the return keyword is added to the method body with an argument of the specified return type.

```
String getPrint()
{
  return "Hello";
}
```

Return is a jump statement that causes the method to exit and return the specified value to the place where the method was called. For example, the method above can be passed as an argument to the getPrint method since the method evaluates to a string.

```
public static void main(String[] args)
{
  MyApp m = new MyApp();
  System.out.print( getPrint() ); // Hello
}
```

The return statement may also be used in void methods to exit before the end block is reached.

```
void myPrint(String s)
{
  System.out.print(s);
}
```

Method overloading

It is possible to declare multiple methods with the same name as long as the parameters vary in type or number. This is called method overloading and can for example be seen in the implementation of the System.out.print method. It is a powerful feature that allows a method to handle a variety of arguments without the programmer needing to be aware of using different methods.

```
void myPrint(String s)
{
  System.out.print(s);
}

void myPrint(int i)
{
  System.out.print(i);
}
```

Passing arguments

Java is different from many other languages in that all method parameters are passed by value. In fact, they cannot be passed by reference. For value data types (primitive types) this means that only a local copy of the variable is changed within the method, so the change will not affect the original variable. For reference data types (classes, interfaces and arrays) it means that only a copy of the memory address is passed to the method. Therefore, if the entire object is replaced the change will not propagate back to the caller, but changes to the object will affect the original since the copy points to the same memory location.

```
public static void main(String[] args)
{
  int x = 0;              // value data type
  m.set(x);               // value is passed
  System.out.print(x);    // 0

  int[] y = {0};          // reference data type
  m.set(y);               // address is passed
  System.out.print(y[0]); // 10
}

void set(int a) { a = 10; }
void set(int[] a) { a[0] = 10; }
```

CHAPTER 10

Class

A class is a template used to create objects. They are made up of members, the main two of which are fields and methods. Fields are variables that hold the state of the object, while methods define what the object can do.

```
class MyRectangle
{
  int x, y;
  int getArea() { return x * y; }
}
```

Object creation

To access a class's fields and methods from outside the defining class, an object of the class must first be created. This is done by using the new keyword, which will create a new object in the system's memory.

```
public class MyApp
{
  public static void main(String[] args)
  {
    // Create an object of MyRectangle
    MyRectangle r = new MyRectangle();
  }
}
```

An object is also called an instance. The object will contain its own set of fields, which can hold values that are different to those of other instances of the class.

Accessing object members

In addition to creating the object, the members of the class that are to be accessible beyond their package need to be declared as public in the class definition.

```
class MyRectangle
{
  public int x, y;
  public int getArea() { return x * y; }
}
```

The members of this object can now be reached by using the dot operator after the instance name.

```
public static void main(String[] args)
{
  MyRectangle r = new MyRectangle();
  r.x = 10;
  r.y = 5;
  int z = r.getArea() // 50 (5*10)
}
```

Constructor

The class can have a constructor. This is a special kind of method used to instantiate (construct) the object. It always has the same name as the class and does not have a return type, since it implicitly returns a new instance of the class. To be accessible from another class not in its package it needs to be declared with the public access modifier. When a new instance of the MyRectangle class is created, by using the new syntax, the constructor method is called, which in the example below sets the fields to some default values.

```
class MyRectangle
{
  int x, y;
  public MyRectangle() { x = 10; y = 20; }

  public static void main(String[] args)
  {
    MyRectangle r = new MyRectangle();
  }
}
```

The constructor can have a parameter list, just as any other method. As seen below, this can be used to make the fields' initial values depend on the parameters passed when the object is created.

```
class MyRectangle
{
  int x, y;
  public MyRectangle(int a, int b) { x = a; y = b; }
```

```
  public static void main(String[] args)
  {
    MyRectangle r = new MyRectangle(20,15);
  }
}
```

This keyword

Inside the constructor, as well as in other methods belonging to the object, a special keyword called this can be used. This keyword is a reference to the current instance of the class. If, for example, the constructor's parameters have the same names as the corresponding fields, then the fields could still be accessed by using the this keyword, even though they are shadowed by the parameters.

```
class MyRectangle
{
  int x, y;
  public MyRectangle(int x, int y)
  {
    this.x = x; this.y = y;
  }
}
```

Constructor overloading

To support different parameter lists the constructor can be overloaded. In the example below, if the class is instantiated without any parameters the fields will be assigned default values. With one parameter both fields will be set to that value, and with two parameters each field will be assigned a separate value. Attempting to create an object with the wrong number of arguments or with incorrect data types will result in a compile-time error, just as with any other method.

```
class MyRectangle
{
  int x, y;
  public MyRectangle()        { x = 10; y = 20; }
  public MyRectangle(int a)       { x = a;  y = a;  }
  public MyRectangle(int a, int b) { x = a;  y = b;  }
}
```

Constructor chaining

The this keyword can also be used to call one constructor from another. This is known as constructor chaining, and allows for greater code reuse. Note that the keyword appears as a method call, and that it must be on the first line in the constructor.

```
public MyRectangle()            { this(10,20);  }
public MyRectangle(int a)       { this(a,a);    }
public MyRectangle(int a, int b) { x = a; y = b; }
```

Initial field values

If there are fields in the class that need to be assigned default values, such as in the first constructor above, the fields can simply be assigned at the same time as they are declared. These initial values will be assigned before the constructor is called.

```
class MyRectangle
{
  int x = 10, y = 20;
}
```

Default constructor

It is possible to create a class even if no constructors are defined. This is because the compiler will then automatically create a default parameterless constructor.

```
class MyClass
{
  public static void main(String[] args)
  {
    // Default constructor used
    MyClass c = new MyClass();
  }
}
```

Null

The built-in constant null is used to represent an uninitialized object. It can only be assigned to objects and not to variables of primitive types. The equal to operator (==) can be used to test whether an object is null.

```
String s = null;
if (s == null) s = new String();
```

Default values

The default value of an object is null. For primitive data types the default values are as follows: numerical types become 0, a char has the Unicode character for zero (\0000) and a boolean is false. Default values will be automatically assigned by the compiler, but only for fields and not for local variables. However, explicitly specifying the default value for fields is considered good programming since it makes the code easier to understand. For local variables the default values will not be set by the compiler. Instead, the compiler forces the programmer to assign values to any local variables that are used, so as to avoid problems associated with using unassigned variables.

```
class MyApp
{
  int x;   // field is assigned default value 0

  int dummy()
  {
    int x; // local variable must be assigned if used
  }
}
```

Garbage collector

The Java runtime environment has a garbage collector that periodically releases the memory used by objects when they are no longer needed. This frees the programmer from the often tedious and error-prone task of memory management. An object will be eligible for destruction when there are no more references to it. This occurs, for example, when the object goes out of scope. An object can also be explicitly dropped by setting its references to null.

Static

The static keyword is used to create fields and methods that can be accessed without having to make an instance of the class. Static (class) members only exist in one copy, which belongs to the class itself, whereas instance (non-static) members are created as new copies for each new object. This means that static methods cannot use instance members since these methods are not part of an instance. On the other hand, instance methods can use both static and instance members.

```
class MyCircle
{
  float r = 10;            // instance field
  static float pi = 3.14F; // static/class field

  // Instance method
  float getArea() { return newArea(r); }

  // Static/class method
  static float newArea(float a) { return pi*a*a; }
}
```

Accessing static members

To access a static member from outside the class, the class name is used followed by the dot operator. This operator is the same as the one used to access instance members, but to reach them an object reference is required. Trying to access a static member by using an object reference (instead of the class name) will give a warning since this makes it more difficult to see that a static member is being used.

```
public static void main(String[] args)
{
  float f = MyCircle.pi;
  MyCircle c = new MyCircle();
  float g = c.r;
}
```

Static methods

The advantage of static members is that they can be used by other classes without having to create an instance of the class. Fields should therefore be declared static when only a single instance of the variable is needed. Methods should be declared static if they perform a generic function that is independent of any instance variables. A good example of this is the Math class which contains only static methods and fields.

```java
double pi = Math.PI;
```

Math is one of the classes that are included by default in every Java application. The reason for this is because it belongs to the java.lang package, which is always imported. This package contains classes fundamental to the Java language, such as: String, Object and System.

Static fields

Static fields have the advantage that they persist throughout the life of the application. They can therefore, for example, be used to record the number of times that a method has been called across all instances of the class. The initial value for a static field will only be set once, sometime before the class or field is ever used.

```java
class MyCircle
{
  static void dummy() { count++; }
  static int count = 0;
}
```

Static initialization blocks

A static initialization block can be used if the initialization of static fields requires more than one line, or some other logic. This block, in contrast to the constructor, will only be run once, at the same time as the static fields are initialized.

```java
static int[] array = new int[5];
static
{
  int i = 0;
  for(int element : array)
    element = i++;
}
```

Instance initialization blocks

An initialization block provides an alternative method for assigning instance fields. This block is placed on the class level, just like the static initialization block, but without the use of the static keyword. Any code placed between the brackets will be copied to the start of every constructor by the compiler.

```
int[] array = new int[5];
{
  int i = 0;
  for(int element : array) element = i++;
}
```

A class can have multiple initialization and static initialization blocks.

■ ■ ■

CHAPTER 12

Inheritance

Inheritance allows a class to acquire the members of another class. In the example below, Apple inherits from Fruit. This is specified with the extends keyword. Fruit then becomes the superclass of Apple, which in turn becomes a subclass of Fruit. In addition to its own members, Apple gains all accessible members in Fruit, except for its constructors.

```
// Superclass (parent class)
class Fruit
{
  public String flavor;
}

// Subclass (child class)
class Apple extends Fruit
{
  public String variety;
}
```

Object

A class in Java may only inherit from one superclass, and if no class is specified it will implicitly inherit from Object. Therefore, Object is the root class of all classes.

```
class Fruit extends Object {}
```

Upcasting

Conceptually, a subclass is a specialization of the superclass. This means that Apple is a kind of Fruit, as well as an Object, and can therefore be used anywhere a Fruit or Object is expected. For example, if an instance of Apple is created, it can be upcast to Fruit since the subclass contains everything in the superclass.

```
Apple a = new Apple();
Fruit f = a;
```

The Apple is then seen as a Fruit, so only the Fruit members can be accessed.

```
f.flavor = "Sweet";
```

Downcasting

When the class is downcast back into an Apple, the fields that are specific to Apple will have been preserved. This is because the Fruit only contained the Apple, it did not convert it. The downcast has to be made explicit since downcasting an actual Fruit into an Apple is not allowed.

```
Apple b = (Apple)f;
```

Instanceof operator

As a safety precaution, you can test to see whether an object can be cast to a specific class by using the `instanceof` operator. This operator returns true if the left side object can be cast into the right side type without causing an exception.

```
Apple c = (f instanceof Apple) ? (Apple)f : null;
```

CHAPTER 13

Overriding

A member in a subclass can redefine a member in its superclass. This is most often done to give instance methods new implementations.

Overriding members

In the example below, Rectangle's getArea method is overridden in Triangle, by redeclaring it there with the same method signature. The signature includes the name, parameters and return type of the method. However, the access level may be changed to allow for more access than the method being overridden.

```
class Rectangle
{
  public int w = 10, h = 10;
  public int getArea() { return w * h; }
}

class Triangle extends Rectangle
{
  public int getArea() { return w * h / 2; }
}
```

Override annotation

In order to show that this override was intentional, the @Override annotation should be placed before the method. This annotation was added in Java 5 to prevent accidental overrides.

```
class Triangle extends Rectangle
{
  @Override public int getArea()
  {
    return w * h / 2;
  }
}
```

Invoking the getArea method from a Triangle instance will call Triangle's version of the method.

```
Triangle o = new Triangle();
o.getArea(); // (50) calls Triangle's version
```

If Triangle's instance is upcast into Rectangle, then Triangle's version of the method will still get called because Rectangle's version has been overridden.

```
Rectangle o = new Triangle();
o.getArea();  // (50) calls Triangle's version
```

Hiding members

This is only true for instance methods, and not for class methods. If a class method called newArea is added to Rectangle, and redefined in Triangle, then Triangle's version of the method will only hide Rectangle's implementation. Because of this the @Override annotation is not used.

```
class Rectangle
{
  public int w = 10, h = 10;
  public static int newArea(int a, int b) {
    return a * b;
  }
}

class Triangle extends Rectangle
{
  public static int newArea(int a, int b) {
    return a * b / 2;
  }
}
```

Calling newArea from Triangle's interface will, as expected, invoke Triangle's version, but calling the method from Rectangle's interface will invoke Rectangle's implementation.

```
Triangle o = new Triangle();
o.newArea(10,10); // (50) calls Triangle's version

Rectangle r = o;
r.newArea(10,10); // (100) calls Rectangle's version
```

Redefined instance methods will always be overridden in Java and redefined class methods will always be hidden. There is no way to change this behavior, as can be done in for example C++ or C#.

Preventing method inheritance

To prevent an instance method from being overridden in subclasses, it can be declared with the `final` method modifier.

```
public final int getArea() { return w * h; }
```

Bear in mind that the order of the method modifiers is not optional. The compiler will point out when the modifiers appear in the wrong order.

Accessing overridden methods

An overridden method can still be accessed from inside the subclass's instance methods by using the super keyword. This keyword is a reference to the current instance of the superclass.

```
@Override public int getArea()
{
  return super.getArea() / 2;
}
```

Calling parent constructor

Another place where the super keyword can be used is on the first line of a constructor. There it can perform a method call that invokes the superclass's constructor.

```
public Triangle(int a, int b) { super(a,b); }
```

If the first line of a constructor is not a call to another constructor, the Java compiler will automatically add a call to the superclass's parameterless constructor. This ensures that all ancestor classes are properly constructed.

```
public Triangle() { super(); }
```

CHAPTER 14

Packages and Import

Packages are used to avoid naming conflicts and to organize code files into different directories. So far in this book the code file has been located at the root of the project's source directory. Therefore, it has belonged to the so called *default package*. In Java, the directory a file belongs to, relative to the project's source directory, corresponds to the package name.

To assign a code file to a package, for example "mypackage", it must be moved to a folder by that name, under the project directory. Furthermore, the file must specify which package it belongs to by using the package keyword followed by the package name (and path). There may only be one package statement in each source file and it must be the first line of code, except for any comments. Note that the naming convention for packages is all lowercase.

```
package mypackage; // this file belongs to mypackage
```

Packages may be any number of directory levels deep and the levels in the hierarchy are separated by dots. For example, if the "mypackage" folder containing the code file is placed in a project folder called "sub", the package declaration would need to look like this:

```
package sub.mypackage;
```

Say this file contains a public class called MyClass. To access MyClass from another source file there are two options. The first is to type the fully qualified name.

```
sub.mypackage.MyClass m;
```

Import specific class

The second option is to shorten the fully qualified name by including the class with the import keyword. An import statement must be located before all other members in the code file, and it has no other purpose than to free the programmer from having to type the fully qualified name.

```
import mypackage.sub.MyClass;
// ...
MyClass m;
```

Import package

In addition to importing a specific class, all types inside of a package can be imported by using an asterisk (*). Note that this does not import any of the subpackages.

```
import java.util.*;
```

Import static

A third variation of the import statement is the static import, which imports all static members of a class. Once the static members are imported, they can be used without having to specify the class name.

```
import static java.lang.Math.*;
// ...
double pi = PI; // Math.PI
```

CHAPTER 15

■ ■ ■

Access Levels

There are four access levels available in Java. These are public, protected, private and package-private. Package-private cannot be explicitly declared by using a keyword. Instead, it is the default access level for every member in Java.

```
public    int myPublic;   // unrestricted access
protected int myProtected;// package or subclass access
          int myPackage;  // package access
private   int myPrivate;  // class access
```

Private access

The most restrictive access level is private. Members with this level can only be used inside of the enclosing (containing) class.

```
package mypackage;
public class MyApp
{
  public    int myPublic;
  protected int myProtected;
            int myPackage;
  private   int myPrivate;

  void test()
  {
    myPublic    = 0; // allowed
    myProtected = 0; // allowed
    myPackage   = 0; // allowed
    myPrivate   = 0; // allowed
  }
}
```

Package-private access

Package-private members can be accessed anywhere within the containing package, but not from another package.

```
package mypackage;
public class MyClass
{
  void test(MyApp m)
  {
    m.myPublic    = 0; // allowed
    m.myProtected = 0; // allowed
    m.myPackage   = 0; // allowed
    m.myPrivate   = 0; // inaccessible
  }
}
```

Protected access

Protected members are accessible within subclasses and within the containing package. Note that the meaning of protected in Java is different from other languages – such as C++ and C# – where protected members are only accessible from subclasses and the containing class.

```
package newpackage;
import mypackage.MyApp;

public class MyClass extends MyApp
{
  void test()
  {
    myPublic    = 0; // allowed
    myProtected = 0; // allowed
    myPackage   = 0; // inaccessible
    myPrivate   = 0; // inaccessible
  }
}
```

Public access

The public modifier gives unrestricted access from anywhere the member can be referenced.

```
package newpackage;
import mypackage.MyApp;
```

```
public class MyClass
{
  void test(MyApp m)
  {
    m.myPublic    = 0; // allowed
    m.myProtected = 0; // inaccessible
    m.myPackage   = 0; // inaccessible
    m.myPrivate   = 0; // inaccessible
  }
}
```

Top-level access

Members declared directly in the package – top-level members – may only choose
between package-private and public access. For instance, a top-level class without an
access modifier will default to package-private. Such a class will only be accessible within
the containing package. On the other hand, a top-level class explicitly declared as public
can be reached from other packages as well.

```
// Accessible only from containing package
class PackagePrivateClass {}

// Accessible from any package
public class PublicClass {}
```

Nested class access

Java allows classes to be defined within other classes, so called nested classes. Such a class
can have any one of the four access levels. If a class is inaccessible, it cannot be instantiated
or inherited.

```
public class MyClass
{
  // Only accessible within MyClass
  private class PrivateNestedClass {}
}
```

Access level guideline

As a guideline, when choosing an access level it is generally best to use the most
restrictive level possible. This is because the more places a member can be accessed the
more places it can be accessed incorrectly, which makes the code harder to debug. Using
restrictive access levels will also make it easier to modify the class without breaking the
code for any other programmers using that class.

.

CHAPTER 16

Constants

A variable in Java can be made into a constant by adding the final keyword before the data type. This modifier means that the variable cannot be reassigned once it has been set, and any attempts to do so will result in a compile-time error.

Local constants

A local constant must always be initialized at the same time as it is declared. The Java naming convention for constants is to use all uppercase letters and to separate the words with underscores.

```
final double PI = 3.14;
```

Constant fields

Class and instance variables can also be declared as final.

```
class MyClass
{
  final double E = 2.72;
  static final double C = 3e8;
}
```

In contrast to local constants, constant fields are not always assigned at declaration. A constant instance field can optionally be assigned in a constructor, and a constant static field may be assigned by using a static initialization block. These alternative assignments can be useful if the constant's value needs to be calculated and does not fit on a single code line.

```
class MyClass
{
  final double E;
  static final double C;
```

```
  public MyClass() { E = 2.72; }
  static { C = 3e8; }
}
```

Constant method parameters

Another place where the final modifier may be applied is to method parameters to make them unchangeable.

```
void f(final int A) {}
```

Compile-time and run-time constants

As in most other languages, Java has both compile-time and run-time constants. However, only class constants can be compile-time constants in Java, and only if their value is known at compilation. All other uses of final will create run-time constants. With compile-time constants the compiler will replace the constant name everywhere in the code with its value. They are therefore faster than run-time constants, which are not set until the program is run. Run-time constants, however, can be assigned dynamic values that can change from one program run to the next.

```
class MyClass
{
  final double E = 2.72;          // run-time constant

  final static double C = 3e8;    // compile-time constant

  final static int RND = (new
  java.util.Random()).nextInt(); // run-time constant
}
```

Constant guideline

In general, it is a good idea to always declare variables as final if they do not need to be reassigned. This ensures that the variables will not be changed anywhere in the program by mistake, which in turn helps to prevent bugs.

CHAPTER 17

Interface

An interface is a type that decouples "interface" from implementation. It specifies a contract between its implementors and objects that call its methods (and access its constants). They are defined with the interface keyword followed by a name and a code block. Their naming convention is the same as for classes, which is to have each word initially capitalized. When an interface is not nested inside another type, its access level can be either package-private or public, just as any other top-level member.

```
interface MyInterface {}
```

Interface members

The code block for an interface can first of all contain signatures for instance methods. These methods cannot have any implementations. Instead, their bodies are replaced by semicolons. Interface members must always be public, and since this is the default access level in interfaces this modifier can be left out.

```
interface MyInterface {
  int myMethod(); // method signature
}
```

The second member that an interface can contain is constants. Any field created in an interface will implicitly be declared as static final, so these modifiers can also be left out.

```
interface MyInterface {
  int c = 10; // constant
}
```

In addition to method signatures and constants, an interface can also contain nested containing types, such as classes or other interfaces.

```
interface MyInterface
{
  // Types
  class Class {}
  interface Interface {}
  enum Enum {}
}
```

Interface example

The example below shows an interface called Comparable, which has a single method named compare.

```
interface Comparable
{
  int compare(Object o);
}
```

The class below implements this interface, by using the `implements` keyword after the class name. By convention, the implements clause is placed after the extends clause, if the class has one. Note that although a class can only inherit from one superclass it may implement any number of interfaces, by specifying them in a comma separated list.

```
class Circle implements Comparable
{
  public int r;
}
```

Because `Circle` implements `Comparable` it must define the `compare` method. For this class the method will return the difference between the circle radiuses. The implemented method must be public, in addition to having the same signature as the method defined in the interface.

```
class Circle implements Comparable
{
  public int r;

  public int compare(Object o) {
    return r - ( (Circle)o ).r;
  }
}
```

Functionality interface

Comparable demonstrates the first usage of interfaces, which is to define a specific functionality that classes can share. It makes it possible to use the interface members without having to know the actual type of a class. To illustrate, the example below shows a simple method that takes two Comparable objects and returns the largest one. This method will work for all classes that implement the Comparable interface regardless of their type, since the method only uses the functionality exposed through that interface.

```
public static Object largest(Comparable a, Comparable b)
{
  return (a.compare(b) > 0) ? a : b;
}
```

Class interface

A second way to use an interface is to provide an actual interface for a class, through which the class can be used. The example below defines an interface for MyClass called MyInterface. This interface only includes the functionality that programmers using MyClass may need.

```
interface MyInterface
{
  void exposed();
}

class MyClass implements MyInterface
{
  public void exposed() {}
  public void hidden() {}
}
```

The interface type is then used to hold the implementing class, so that the class is only seen through this interface.

```
public static void main(String[] args)
{
  MyInterface i = new MyClass();
}
```

This abstraction provides two benefits. First, it makes it easier for other programmers to use the class since they now only have access to the methods that are relevant. Second, it makes the class more flexible since its implementation can change, without being noticeable by other programmers using the class, as long as the interface is followed.

Interface classes

As mentioned previously, an interface can contain nested types, such as classes. In contrast to methods, these types are implemented inside the interface. This can, for example, be used to provide a class that contains static methods useful for implementing classes. These nested types are only visible to classes implementing the interface, and not to objects of those classes.

```
interface MyInterface
{
  class HelperClass {
    public static void helperMethod() {}
  }
}
```

CHAPTER 18

Abstract

An abstract class provides a partial implementation that other classes can build upon. When a class is declared as abstract it means that the class can contain incomplete methods that must be implemented in subclasses, in addition to normal class members. These methods are left unimplemented and only specify their signatures, while their bodies are replaced by semicolons.

```
abstract class Shape
{
  public int x = 100, y = 100;
  public abstract int getArea();
}
```

Abstract class example

If a class called Rectangle inherits from the abstract class Shape, Rectangle is then forced to override the abstract getArea method. The only exception is if Rectangle is also declared abstract, in which case it does not have to implement any abstract methods.

```
class Rectangle extends Shape
{
  @Override public int getArea()
  {
    return x * y;
  }
}
```

An abstract class cannot be instantiated, but it can be used to hold instances of its subclasses.

```
Shape s = new Rectangle();
```

Even though an abstract class cannot be instantiated it may have constructors, which can be called from the subclass's constructors by using the super keyword.

```
abstract class Shape
{
  public int x = 100, y = 100;
  public Shape(int a, int b) { x = a; y = b; }
}

class Rectangle extends Shape
{
  public Rectangle(int a, int b) { super(a,b); }
}
```

Abstract classes and interfaces

Abstract classes are similar to interfaces in many ways. They can both define method signatures that subclasses must implement, and neither one of them can be instantiated. The key differences are first that the abstract class can contain non-abstract members, while the interface cannot. And second, that a class can implement any number of interfaces but only inherit from one class, abstract or not. Note that an abstract class can, just as a non-abstract class, extend one superclass and implement any number of interfaces. An interface, however, cannot inherit from a class. Although it can extend another interface, which effectively combines the two interfaces into one.

Abstract class and interface guideline

An interface is either used to define a specific functionality that a class can have, or to provide an interface for other programmers using a class. An abstract class on the other hand is used to provide a partial class implementation, leaving it up to subclasses to complete it. This is useful when subclasses have a lot of functionality in common, but also have some functionality that must be implemented differently for each subclass.

CHAPTER 19

Enum

An enumeration is a type that consists of a fixed list of named constants. To create one, the enum keyword is used followed by a name and a code block, containing a comma separated list of constant elements. The access level for an enumeration is the same as for a class. Package-private by default, but it can also be set to public if it is declared in a file of the same name. Just as with classes, an enumeration can be contained within a class, where it can then be set to any access level.

```
enum Speed
{
  STOP, SLOW, NORMAL, FAST
}
```

An object of the enum type above can hold any one of the four defined constants. The enum constants are accessed as if they were static fields of a class.

```
Speed s = Speed.SLOW;
```

Enum example

The switch statement provides a good example of when an enumeration can be useful. Compared to using ordinary constants, an enumeration has the advantage of allowing the programmer to clearly specify what constant values are allowed. This provides compile-time type safety. Note that when using an enum in a switch statement, the case labels are not qualified with the name of the enum.

```
switch(s) { case SLOW: break; }
```

Enum class

In Java, the enum type is more powerful than its counterparts in other languages, such as C++ or C#. It is essentially a special kind of class, and can include anything that a class can include. To add a class member the list of constants must be terminated with a semicolon, and the member must be declared after the constants. In the example below, an integer is added to the enum, which will hold the actual speed that the elements represent.

```
enum Speed
{
  STOP, SLOW, NORMAL, FAST;
  public int speed;
}
```

To set this field, a constructor needs to be added as well. A constructor in an enumeration must have either private or package-private access and is not called in the same way as for a regular class. Instead, the parameters to the constructor are given after the constant elements, as seen below. For example, if a Speed enum object is assigned the constant SLOW, then the argument 5 will be passed to the constructor for that enum instance.

```
enum Speed
{
  STOP(0), SLOW(5), NORMAL(10), FAST(20);
  public int speed;

  Speed(int s) { speed = s; }
}
```

Another difference that enum types have when compared to regular classes, is that they implicitly extend from the java.lang.Enum class. In addition to the members inherited from this class, the compiler will also automatically add two static methods to the enumeration, namely values and valueof. The values method returns an array of the constant elements declared in the enum, and valueof returns the enum constant of the specified enum name.

```
Speed[] a = Speed.values();
Speed s = Speed.valueOf(a[0].toString()); // Speed.STOP
```

■ ■ ■

CHAPTER 20

Exception Handling

Exception handling allows programmers to deal with unexpected situations that may occur in their programs. As an example, the FileReader class in the java.io package is used to open a file. Creating an instance of this class will cause Netbeans to give a reminder that the class's constructor may throw a FileNotFoundException. Attempting to run the program will also cause the compiler to point this out.

```
import java.io.*;
// ...
FileReader in = new FileReader("Missing.file"); // error
```

Try-catch

To get rid of this compile-time error the exception must be caught by using a try-catch statement. This statement consists of a try block containing the code that may cause the exceptions, and one or more catch clauses. If the try block executes successfully the program will continue running after the try-catch statement, but if an exception occurs, execution will then be passed to the first catch block able to handle that exception type.

```
import java.io.*;
// ...
try {
  FileReader in = new FileReader("Missing.file");
}
catch(FileNotFoundException e) {}
```

Catch block

In the example above, the catch block is only set to handle the FileNotFoundException. If the code in the try block could throw more kinds of exceptions, and all of them should be handled in the same way, a more general exception can be caught instead, such as the Exception class itself. This catch clause would then be able to handle all the exceptions that inherit from this class, including the FileNotFoundException. Bear in mind that a more general exception needs to be caught after a more specific exception. The catch clause must always define an exception object. This object can be used to obtain more information about the exception, such as a description of the exception by using the getMessage method.

```
catch(FileNotFoundException e) {
  System.out.print(e.getMessage());
}
catch(Exception e) {
  System.out.print(e.getMessage());
}
```

Finally block

As the last clause in a try-catch statement, a finally block can be added. This block is used to clean up resources allocated in the try block and will always execute whether or not there is an exception. In this example, the file opened in the try block should be closed, but only if it was successfully opened. To be able to access the FileReader object from the finally clause it must be declared outside of the try block. Additionally, because the close method can also throw an exception it needs to be surrounded with another try-catch block. Keep in mind that if you forget to close a file Java's garbage collector will eventually do it for you, but it is a good programming practice to do it yourself.

```
import java.io.*;
// ...
FileReader in = null;
try {
  in = new FileReader("Missing.file");
}
catch(FileNotFoundException e) {
  System.out.print(e.getMessage());
}
finally {
  if (in != null) {
    try { in.close(); }
    catch(IOException e) {}
  }
}
```

Throwing exceptions

When a situation occurs that a method cannot recover from, it can generate its own exception to signal to the caller that the method has failed. This is done by using the throw keyword followed by a new instance of a Throwable type.

```
static void MakeException()
{
  throw new Throwable("My Throwable");
}
```

Checked and unchecked exceptions

Exceptions in Java are grouped into two categories – checked and unchecked – depending on whether or not they need to be specified. A method that throws a checked exception, for example IOException, will not compile unless it is specified by using a throws clause after the method's parameter list and the calling method catches the exception. Unchecked exceptions on the other hand, such as the ArithmeticException, do not have to be caught or specified. Note that to specify multiple exceptions the exception types are separated by a comma.

```
import java.io.*;
// ...
static void MakeException() throws IOException,
                                    ArithmeticException
{
  throw new IOException("My IO exception");
  // ...
  throw new ArithmeticException("Division by zero");
}
```

Exception hierarchy

Exceptions, like most everything else in Java, are classes that exist in a hierarchy. At the root of this hierarchy (below Object) is the Throwable class, and all descendants of this class can be both thrown and caught. Inheriting from Throwable there are the Error and Exception classes. Classes descending from Error are used to indicate non-recoverable exceptions, such as the OutOfMemoryError. These are unchecked because once they have occurred it is unlikely that the programmer can do anything about them even if they are caught.

Descending from Exception are the RuntimeExceptions, which are also unchecked. These are exceptions that can occur in almost any code, and it would therefore be cumbersome to catch and specify them. For example, a division by zero will throw an ArithmeticException, however surrounding every division operation with a try-catch would be bothersome. There is also an overhead associated with checking for exceptions and the cost of checking for these exceptions outweighs the benefit of catching them. The other Exception descendants, those that do not inherit from RuntimeExceptions, are all checked. These are exceptions that can be recovered from and that must be both caught and specified.

CHAPTER 21

Boxing and Unboxing

Placing a primitive variable in an object is known as boxing. This allows the primitive to be used where objects are required. For this purpose Java provides wrapper classes for each primitive – namely: Byte, Short, Integer, Long, Float, Double, Character and Boolean. An Integer object, for example, can hold a variable of the type int.

```
int iPrimitive = 5;
Integer iWrapper = new Integer(iPrimitive); // boxing
```

The opposite of boxing is unboxing. This converts the object type back into its primitive type.

```
iPrimitive = iWrapper.intValue(); // unboxing
```

The wrapper classes belong to the java.lang package, which is always imported. In contrast to primitives, wrapper objects are immutable (unchangeable). To change their value, a new instance must be created. Another difference between primitives and wrapper objects is how they are checked for equality. Primitives use the equal to operator (==), whereas objects of any type use the equals method, extending from Object. Also bear in mind that objects can be set to null whereas primitives cannot.

Autoboxing and autounboxing

Java 5 introduced autoboxing and autounboxing. These features allow for automatic conversion between primitives and their wrapper objects.

```
Integer iWrapper = iPrimitive; // autoboxing
iPrimitive = iWrapper;         // autounboxing
```

Note that this is only syntactic sugar designed to make the code easier to read. The compiler will add the necessary code to box and unbox the primitives for you – using the valueOf and intValue methods.

```
Integer iWrapper = Integer.valueOf(iPrimitive);
iPrimitive = iWrapper.intValue()
```

Primitive and wrapper guideline

Primitive types should be used when there is no need for objects. This is because primitives are generally faster and more memory efficient than objects. Conversely, wrappers are useful when numerical values are needed, but objects are required. For example, to store numerical values in a collection class, such as ArrayList, the wrapper classes are needed.

```java
java.util.ArrayList a = new java.util.ArrayList();
a.add(Integer.valueOf(5)); // boxing
a.add(10);                 // autoboxing
```

Bear in mind that conversions between primitives and wrapper objects should be kept low if speed is important. There is an inherit performance penalty associated with any boxing and unboxing operation.

CHAPTER 22

Generics

Generics refer to the use of type parameters, which provide a way to define methods, classes and interfaces that can operate with different data types. The benefits of generics is that they provide compile-time type safety, and that they eliminate the need for most type conversions.

Generic classes

Generic classes allow class members to use type parameters. Such a class is defined by adding a type parameter section after the class name, which contains a type parameter enclosed between angle brackets. The naming convention for type parameters is that they should consist of a single uppercase letter. Typically, the letter T for type is used. The example below defines a generic container class that can hold a single element of the generic type.

```
// Generic container class
class MyBox<T> { public T box; }
```

When an object of this generic class is instantiated, the type parameter must be replaced with an actual data type, such as Integer.

```
MyBox<Integer> iBox = new MyBox<Integer>();
```

Alternatively, as of Java 7, a generic class can be instantiated with an empty set of type parameters. This type of instantiation is possible as long as the compiler can infer (determine) the type parameters from the context.

```
MyBox<Integer> iBox = new MyBox<>();
```

When an instance of MyBox is created, each type parameter in the class definition is replaced with the passed in type argument. The object therefore behaves as a regular object, with a single field of the Integer type.

```
iBox.box = 5;
Integer i = iBox.box;
```

Notice that no casting is required when the stored value is set or retrieved from the box field. Furthermore, if the generic field is mistakenly assigned to or set to an incompatible type, the compiler will point this out.

```
iBox.box = "Hello World"; // compile-time error
String s = iBox.box;      // compile-time error
```

Generic methods

A method can be made generic by declaring it with a type parameter section before the method's return type. The type parameter can be used as any other type inside of the method. It can also be used for the method's return type, in the throws clause and for its parameter types. The example below shows a generic class method that accepts a generic array parameter, the content of which is printed out.

```
class MyClass
{
  public static <T> void printArray(T[] array)
  {
    for (T element : array)
      System.out.print(element + " ");
  }
}
```

Methods can be declared as generic, independently of whether or not the enclosing class or interface is generic. The same is true for constructors.

Calling generic methods

A generic method is typically invoked just as a regular (non-generic) method, without specifying the type argument.

```
Integer[] iArray = { 1, 2, 3 };
MyClass.printArray(iArray);
```

In most cases, the Java compiler can infer the type argument of a generic method call, and so it does not have to be included. However, if this is not the case the type argument will then need to be explicitly specified.

```
MyClass.<Integer>printArray(iArray);
```

Generic interfaces

Interfaces that are declared with type parameters become generic interfaces. Generic interfaces have the same two purposes as regular interfaces. They are either created to expose members of a class that will be used by other classes, or to force a class to implement a specific functionality. When a generic interface is implemented, the type argument must be specified. The generic interface can be implemented by both generic and non-generic classes.

```
// Generic functionality interface
interface IGenericCollection<T>
{
  public void store(T t);
}

// Non-generic class implementing generic interface
class Box implements IGenericCollection<Integer>
{
  public Integer myBox;
  public void store(Integer i) { myBox = i; }
}

// Generic class implementing generic interface
class GenericBox<T> implements IGenericCollection<T>
{
  public T myBox;
  public void store(T t) { myBox = t; }
}
```

Generic type parameters

The passed in type argument for a generic can either be a class type, interface type or another type parameter. It cannot, however, be a primitive type. Generics can have more than one type parameter defined, just by adding more of them between the angle brackets in a comma-separated list. Bear in mind that each parameter within the brackets must be unique.

```
class MyClass<T, U> {}
```

If a generic has multiple type parameters defined, the same number of type arguments need to be specified when the generic is used.

```
MyClass<Integer, Float> myClass = new MyClass<Integer,
                                     Float>();
```

Generic variable usages

Generics are only a compile-time construct in Java. After the compiler has checked that the types used with generic variables are correct, it will then erase all type parameter and argument information from the generic code and insert the appropriate casts instead. This means that generics do not give any performance benefits over non-generic code, because of removed run-time casts, as they do in for example C#. It also means that generic types cannot be used for anything that requires run-time information – such as creating new instances of generic types or using the instanceof operator with type parameters. Operations that are allowed include: declaring variables of the generic type, assigning null to generic variables and calling Object methods.

```
class MyClass<T>
{
  public void myMethod(Object o)
  {
    T t1;                          // allowed
    t1 = null;                     // allowed
    System.out.print(t1.toString()); // allowed
    if (o instanceof T) {}         // invalid
    T t2 = new T();                // invalid
  }
}
```

The process of removing type information from generic code is known as *type erasure*. For example, MyBox<Integer> would be reduced to MyBox, which is called the *raw type*. This step is performed in order to maintain backwards compatibility with code written before generics became part of the language in Java 5.

Bounded type parameters

It is possible to apply compile-time enforced restrictions on the kinds of type parameters that a generic may be used with. These restrictions are called *bounds*, and they are specified within the type parameter section by using the extends keyword. Type parameters can be bounded by either superclass or interface. For example, the class B below may only be instantiated with a type argument that either is of the type A, or has that class as a superclass.

```
// T must be or inherit from superclass A
class B<T extends A> {}
class A {}
```

The second example specifies an interface as the bound. This will restrict the type parameter to only those types that implement the specified interface, or are of the interface type itself.

```
// T must be or implement interface I
class C<T extends I> {}
interface I {}
```

Multiple bounds can be applied to a type parameter by specifying them in a list separated by ampersands.

```
class D<T extends A & I> {}
```

The ampersand acts as the separator instead of a comma since comma is already used for separating type parameters.

```
class E<T extends A & I, U extends A & I> {}
```

Aside from restricting the use of a generic to only certain parameter types, another reason for applying bounds is to increase the number of permitted method calls supported by the bounded type. An unbounded type may only call the Object methods. However, by applying a superclass or interface bound, the accessible members of that type will also become available.

```
class Fruit
{
  public String name;
}

class FruitBox<T extends Fruit>
{
  private T box;
  public void FruitBox(T t) { box = t; }
  public String getFruitName()
  {
    // Use of Fruit member allowed since T extends Fruit
    return box.name;
  }
}
```

Generics and Object

Before generics were introduced in Java 5, the Object type was used to create container classes that could store any type of objects. Now that generics are available, this use of the Object type as a universal container should be avoided. This is because the compiler helps ensure that generics are type safe at compile-time, which cannot be done when using the Object type.

The collection classes in the Java library, among them ArrayList, have all been replaced with generic versions. Even so, any generic class can still be used as if it was not generic, simply by leaving out the type argument section. The default Object type will then be used as the type argument. This is the reason why the non-generic version of ArrayList is still allowed. Consider the following use of a non-generic ArrayList.

```
import java.util.ArrayList;
// ...
// Object ArrayList
ArrayList a = new ArrayList();
a.add("Hello World");
// ...
Integer b = (Integer)a.get(0); // run-time error
```

This String to Integer conversion will fail at run-time by throwing a ClassCastException. Had a generic ArrayList been used instead, the mistaken conversion would have been detected upon compilation, or immediately in an IDE such as Netbeans.

```
import java.util.ArrayList;
// ...
// Generic ArrayList (recommended)
ArrayList<String> a = new ArrayList<String>();
a.add("Hello World");
// ...
Integer b = (Integer)a.get(0); // compile-time error
```

With the generic alternative only the specified type argument will be allowed into the ArrayList collection. Additionally, values obtained from the collection do not have to be cast to the correct type since the compiler takes care of that.

Index

A

abstract, 57
Access levels, 47
Anonymous block, 8
Array(s), 15
ArrayList, 16
assignment operator (=), 6, 9

B

boolean, 7
Bounds, 70
Boxing, 65
break, 22
byte, 6

C

catch, 61
char, 7
class, 29
class member, 35
code block, 2
comma operator (,), 6, 22
Comments, 4
compile, 3
concatenation operator (+), 13
Conditionals, 19
constant, 51
Constructor, 30
continue, 22

D

Data types, 5
declare, 5
decrement operator ( ), 10

default constructor, 32
define, 6
dot operator (.), 2, 30
double, 7
do-while, 21
downcast, 40

E

enclosing class, 47
enum, 59
Escape characters, 13
Exception handling, 61
Exception hierarchy, 63
extends, 39, 70

F

false, 10
field, 29
final, 43, 51
finally, 62
float, 7
for, 21
foreach, 22

G

Garbage collector, 33
Generics, 67

H

Hello world, 1

I

IDE, 1
if, 19

import, 45
increment operator (++), 10
Inheritance, 39
Initialization block, 37
initialize, 6
Instance, 29
Instance member, 35
instanceof operator, 40
instantiate, 30
int, 6
Interface, 53
invoke, 25
iteration, 21

J, K

java.lang, 36
JDK, 1

L

Labeled block, 23
logical and (&&), 11
logical not (!), 11
logical or (||), 11
long, 6
loops, 21

M

Main method, 2
Method(s), 25
Method overloading, 27
modulus operator (%), 9
Multi-dimensional arrays, 16

N

nested class, 49
new, 29
null, 32

O

Object, 29, 39
Operators, 9
@Override, 41
Overriding, 41

P, Q

Package, 45
Package-private, 48
Primitives, 5
print, 2
private, 47
protected, 48
public, 48

R

return, 26

S

Scope, 8
semicolon (;), 2
short, 6
signature, 41
static, 35
String, 13
StringBuffer, 14
super, 43
switch, 20

T

ternary operator (?:), 20
this, 31
throw, 62
Top-level member, 49
true, 10
try, 61

U

Unboxing, 65
Upcast, 39

V

Variables, 5
void, 25

W, X, Y, Z

while, 21
Wrapper classes, 65